Essential COOKING SERIES

COMPREHENSIVE, STEP-BY-STEP COOKING

Pasta Dishes

HINKLER
BOOKS

Essential Cooking Series: Pasta Dishes
First published in 2009 by Hinkler Books Pty Ltd
45–55 Fairchild Street
Heatherton Victoria 3202 Australia
www.hinklerbooks.com

Disclaimer: The nutritional information listed under each recipe does not include the nutrient content of garnishes or any accompaniments not listed in specific quantitites in the ingredient list. The nutritional information for each recipe is an estimate only, and may vary depending on the brand of ingredients used, and due to natural biological variations in the composition of natural foods such as meat, fish, fruit and vegetables. The nutritional information was calculated by using Foodworks dietary analysis software (Version 3, Xyris Software Pty Ltd, Highgate Hill, Queensland, Australia) based on the Australian food composition tables and food manufacturers' data. Where not specified, ingredients are always analysed as average or medium, not small or large.

ISBN: 978 1 7418 5709 2

10 9 8 7 6 5 4 3
14 13 12 11 10

Printed and bound in China

Contents

An introduction to pasta dishes

With great ease, pasta can be transformed into low-cost, versatile, healthy and tasty meals. For a quiet night at home, dinner can be as simple as tossing a garlic and tomato sauce through spaghetti. An impressive meal of fresh seafood on pappardelle with a creamy saffron sauce can be served to dinner-party guests. Or the salad table at a barbecue can be enriched with a hot or cold pasta salad laden with fresh herbs and roasted capsicums (peppers).

PASTA SHAPES

In Italy, pasta is available in hundreds of exciting shapes. Most pasta is known by its Italian name. The literal translation of these names can hint at a pasta's shape: cannelloni or tubes; conchigle or conch shells; fusilli or spindles; gemelli or twins; linguine or little tongues; penne or quills; ravioli or turnips; spaghetti or strings; tagliatelle or ribbons; tortellini or tarts; and vermicelli or little worms.

What shape when?

Choosing the right pasta for a sauce is a common dilemma. Fortunately, there are no hard and fast rules. A good guide is to remember that hollow tube pastas such a penne and rigatoni are good for chunky, thicker sauces, while thinner, flatter pastas such as linguine and fettuccine are better suited to smoother creamy sauces.

FRESH OR DRIED?

Most of the recipes in this book call for dried pasta, but fresh pasta can be used instead. Fresh pasta will usually absorb more of the sauce than dried pasta, so you will need to take this into consideration – it can become quite soggy when served with a wet tomato sauce, but is perfect when tossed with a simple pesto. Fresh pasta tends to be softer than dried, so it will not hold its shape when cooked. For this reason it would be better to choose dried pasta for chunkier seafood or vegetable sauces.

Flours

Pasta is made by combining flour with water; often it will be enriched with oil or egg. Look for durum wheat pasta, as it is considered to be the finest quality flour for pasta-making. If you are intolerant to gluten there are a large variety of rice, potato, corn and buckwheat pastas available in the health section of your supermarket or from the local health food store.

Storage
Dried pasta will last for up to 6 months stored in an airtight container away from direct sunlight. Fresh pasta can be stored in the refrigerator for up to 5 days, or frozen for up to 4 months if securely wrapped in a double layer of plastic.

Do not thaw before cooking, simply add straight to the pan from the freezer.

QUANTITIES
How much pasta should you cook? As a rule, men will usually eat more than women, and adults more than children. However, it is always better to serve too much rather than too little. The following is a rough guideline to quantities of uncooked pasta per person:

Entrée
fresh pasta 60–80 g per person
dried pasta 90–100 g per person

Mains
fresh pasta 100–125 g per person
dried pasta 125–150 g per person

COOKING PASTA

Pasta is easy to cook. Firstly, you need a good-sized pot for boiling the water. If the pot is too small, the pasta will clump together and glue itself to the bottom of the pan. If you choose to cook your pasta in salted water, don't add the salt until the water has boiled, as unsalted water will reach boiling point much faster. Covering the pot will also help it to boil more quickly. Once the water has boiled, add the pasta and stir it a couple of times to start the pasta moving in the water. Cover the pan and allow it to return to the boil. Remove the lid as soon as it reaches the boil or the water will overflow onto the stovetop.

Cook the pasta until it is al dente, which is Italian for 'the tooth'. It should be soft but still slightly firm. Once cooked, drain the pasta in a large metal colander. There is no need to rinse it under cold water unless it is going to be used to make pasta salad. Do not over-drain the pasta, as this will make it sticky. Pasta should be served as soon as it has been cooked – if left to stand it will form a solid mass. If you are making a pasta salad and need to cool the pasta, toss through a little olive oil to keep the pasta separate. It is best to prepare the sauce before you cook the pasta.

The cooking time will vary depending on the brand, so be sure to read the manufacturer's instructions. Fresh pasta takes less time to cook than dried and should not be overcooked or it will break up. Fresh gnocchi will float to the surface of the pot when it is cooked and it should be removed from the pan using a slotted spoon.

Pasta with pumpkin and sage butter

INGREDIENTS

2 tablespoons olive oil
2 cloves garlic, crushed
2 tablespoon chopped fresh sage
1 butternut pumpkin, cubed
400 g (13 oz) dried penne
90 g (3 oz) butter
30 g (1 oz) pine nut kernels
30 g (1 oz) parmesan, grated
salt and black pepper
extra sage to garnish
serves 4

PREPARATION TIME
15 minutes

COOKING TIME
30 minutes

1 Preheat oven to 230°C (450°F, gas mark 8). Combine oil, garlic, 1 tablespoon of sage and the butternut pumpkin. Cook in oven for 20 minutes until tender.

2 Cook pasta in a large pan of boiling water until al dente, then drain, reserving 1 cup of water.

3 Melt butter in a large frying pan, add remaining chopped sage, and cook gently for 2–3 minutes. Put pine nuts on a baking tray, place in oven and toast until golden.

4 Add the reserved cooking liquid to the butter. Add pasta and cooked pumpkin. Toss and serve sprinkled with the parmesan, pine nuts and pepper. Garnish with fresh sage.

NUTRITIONAL VALUE PER SERVE	FAT 10.7 G	CARBOHYDRATE 23 G	PROTEIN 6 G

Wholewheat spaghetti with four cheeses

INGREDIENTS

400 g (13 oz) dried wholewheat
  spaghetti
90 g (3 oz) butter
60 g (2 oz) parmesan, grated
90 g (3 oz) gruyère, cut into thin
  strips
90 g (3 oz) bel paese, cut into thin
  strips
125 g (4 oz) mozzarella, cut into
  chunks
salt and black pepper
serves 4

PREPARATION TIME
20 minutes

COOKING TIME
**25 minutes, plus
15 minutes standing**

1 Preheat oven to 200°C (400°F, gas mark 6). Cook pasta in a large
   pan of boiling water until al dente, and drain. Return to pan, toss
   with half the butter and half the parmesan. Add gruyère, bel
   paese, mozzarella and pepper, and mix well to combine.

2 Transfer pasta and cheese mixture to a greased ovenproof dish.
   Dot with remaining butter. Sprinkle with remaining parmesan.
   Bake for 10–15 minutes, until top is crisp and golden. Leave to
   stand for 15 minutes before serving.

NUTRITIONAL VALUE PER SERVE   FAT 21.7 G   CARBOHYDRATE 28 G   PROTEIN 16.1 G

Thick minestrone with pesto

INGREDIENTS

3 tablespoons olive oil
1 onion, chopped
2 cloves garlic, crushed
1 potato, cubed
2 small carrots, cubed
1 large courgette (zucchini), cubed
¼ white cabbage, chopped
700 ml (1¼ pints) vegetable stock
2 x 400 g (13 oz) cans tomatoes,
  chopped
75 g (2½ oz) pasta shells
salt and black pepper
4 tablespoons grated parmesan
4 tablespoons pesto
serves 4

PREPARATION TIME
15 minutes

COOKING TIME
45 minutes

1 Place oil in a large pan, add onion, garlic, potato, carrots, courgette (zucchini) and cabbage. Cook for 5–7 minutes, until softened.

2 Add stock and tomatoes and bring to the boil. Reduce heat and simmer for 20 minutes, add pasta shells and seasoning. Cook for a further 10 minutes, until pasta is al dente. Divide soup between bowls and top each serving with a tablespoon of parmesan and pesto.

| NUTRITIONAL VALUE PER SERVE | FAT 3.9 G | CARBOHYDRATE 15 G | PROTEIN 2 G |

Fusilli with capsicums and sun-dried tomatoes

INGREDIENTS

1 large red capsicum (pepper)
1 large yellow capsicum (pepper)
$^{1}/_{2}$ cup (125 ml, 4 fl oz) extra virgin
   olive oil
2 shallots, finely chopped
1 clove garlic, crushed
1 teaspoon dried chillies, crushed
$^{1}/_{2}$ cup (125 ml, 4 fl oz) vegetable stock
125 g (4 oz) sun-dried tomatoes in oil,
   drained and chopped
2 tablespoons capers, rinsed and dried
2 tablespoons balsamic vinegar
400 g (13 oz) dried fusilli
2 tablespoons chopped fresh oregano
serves 4

PREPARATION TIME
15 minutes

COOKING TIME
45 minutes

1 Preheat grill to high. Grill capsicums (peppers) until skin blackens and blisters. Transfer to a plastic bag to cool; remove skins, deseed and chop.

2 Heat half the oil in a large pan, add shallots and cook for 5 minutes until softened. Add garlic, chillies and 2 tablespoons of the stock. Cook for 5 minutes, add capsicums (peppers) and sun-dried tomatoes. Cook for a further 10 minutes, adding more stock if needed. Stir in capers and vinegar and cook for 1 minute.

3 Cook pasta in a large pan of boiling water, until al dente. Drain and toss with remaining oil. Spoon over the sauce, mix to combine. Serve hot or cold, garnished with oregano.

NUTRITIONAL VALUE PER SERVE	FAT 11.5 G	CARBOHYDRATE 29 G	PROTEIN 6.2 G

Pasta with goat's cheese and asparagus

INGREDIENTS

1 tablespoon sunflower oil
2 tablespoons butter
2 red onions, thinly sliced
1 clove garlic, crushed
400 g (13 oz) dried pasta, such
   as penne
250 g (8 oz) bunch asparagus,
   trimmed and cut into small pieces
150 g (5 oz) peas, fresh or frozen
100 g (3¹/₂ oz) goat's cheese, crumbled
sea salt and freshly ground
   black pepper
serves 4

PREPARATION TIME
15 minutes

COOKING TIME
20 minutes

1 Heat oil and butter in a frying pan, and cook onion over a medium heat for 7 minutes, stirring occasionally. Add garlic and cook for a further 3 minutes, until golden and crisp.

2 Bring a large pan of water to the boil. Add pasta and cook for 5 minutes, add asparagus and cook for a further 2 minutes, add peas and cook for further 2 minutes. Drain well.

3 Return pasta and vegetables to the pan, add most of the onion. Add goat's cheese, sea salt and black pepper, mix to combine. Serve topped with the remaining onions.

NUTRITIONAL VALUE PER SERVE	FAT **6.3** G	CARBOHYDRATE **27** G	PROTEIN **7.1** G

Vegetarian lasagne

INGREDIENTS

2 tablespoons oil
1 large aubergine (eggplant), cubed
125 g (4 oz) mushrooms, sliced
1 carrot, grated
1 courgette (zucchini), grated
500 g (1 lb) jar tomato pasta sauce
140 g (4$^1/_2$ oz) tomato paste
1 cup (250 ml, 8 fl oz) water
$^1/_2$ cup (125 ml, 4 fl oz) red wine
2 tablespoons chopped fresh parsley
butter for greasing
250 g (8 oz) instant lasagne sheets
200 g (7 oz) ricotta cheese
250 g (8 oz) mozzarella, grated
serves 4–6

PREPARATION TIME
30 minutes

COOKING TIME
1 hour, plus
10 minutes
standing

1   Preheat oven to 190°C (375°F, gas mark 5). In a large pan, heat oil, add aubergine (eggplant), mushrooms, carrot and courgette (zucchini) and cook on a medium-high heat for 2–3 minutes. Stir in pasta sauce, tomato paste, water, wine and parsley. Cover, reduce heat and simmer for 15 minutes, stirring occasionally.

2   Grease a 20 x 30 cm (8 in x 12 in) ovenproof dish with butter and spread $^1/_3$ of vegetable sauce over base. Cover with a layer of lasagne sheets. Spread $^1/_3$ of ricotta onto pasta and sprinkle with $^1/_3$ cup mozzarella.

3   Repeat the layers twice, finishing with ricotta and sprinkling with a cup of mozzarella cheese.

4   Bake for 30–40 minutes, until golden and bubbling. Allow to stand for 10 minutes before serving.

NUTRITIONAL VALUE PER SERVE	FAT 5.9 G	CARBOHYDRATE 12 G	PROTEIN 6.2 G

Gnocchi with thyme

INGREDIENTS

3 tablespoons olive oil
500 g (1 lb) fresh potato gnocchi
1 red capsicum (pepper)
100 g (3½ oz) butter
15 g (½ oz) fresh thyme leaves
3 tablespoons chopped fresh parsley
55 g (2 oz) roasted pecans or walnuts
serves 4

1 Preheat grill to high. Heat oil in a large pan until very hot. Add gnocchi, cook gently until golden brown. Drain on kitchen paper and set aside.

2 Cut capsicum (pepper) into 4 and press flat onto grilling tray, skin side up. Cook until skin blisters and blackens. Remove, place in a plastic bag and seal until cool. Remove skin and cut into strips.

3 Heat butter in a large pan, add herbs and sauté for 1 minute. Add gnocchi and pecans (or walnuts), and toss to heat through. Serve topped with char-grilled capsicums (peppers).

PREPARATION TIME
15 minutes

COOKING TIME
25 minutes

| NUTRITIONAL VALUE PER SERVE | FAT **20.8** G | CARBOHYDRATE **17** G | PROTEIN **3.7** G |

Spaghetti carbonara

INGREDIENTS

185 g (6 oz) sliced ham, cut into
  strips
4 eggs
1/3 cup (90 ml, 3 fl oz) single cream
90 g (3 oz) parmesan, grated
500 g (1 lb) dried spaghetti
freshly ground black pepper
serves 4

1 Heat a non-stick frying pan and cook ham
a medium heat for 2–3 minutes. Place eggs,
cream and parmesan in a large bowl and beat
lightly to combine. Set aside.

2 Cook spaghetti in a large pan of boiling water
until al dente. Place spaghetti in a large serving
dish while still hot, add egg mixture and ham
and toss, allowing the heat of the spaghetti to
cook the sauce. Season with black pepper and
serve.

PREPARATION TIME
15 minutes

COOKING TIME
20 minutes

NUTRITIONAL VALUE PER SERVE	FAT 9.5 G	CARBOHYDRATE 40 G	PROTEIN 15.2 G

with bolognese

2 tablespoons butter
115 g (4 oz) pancetta or bacon,
  roughly chopped
1 small onion, finely diced
1 small carrot, finely diced
1 stick celery, finely diced
1 clove garlic, crushed
400 g (13 oz) minced beef
1/2 cup (125 ml, 4 fl oz) dry white wine
2 tablespoons tomato purée
1/2 cup (125 ml, 4 fl oz) beef stock
salt and pepper
milk, to moisten
500 g (1 lb) fresh tagliatelle
parmesan, grated
serves 4

PREPARATION TIME
20 minutes

COOKING TIME
2 hours and
50 minutes

1 Place oil, butter, pancetta or bacon, onion, carrot, celery and garlic in a large pan
   and cook over a low heat for 5–7 minutes, until vegetables have softened, stirring
   occasionally. Add mince and cook for 3–5 minutes, until browned.

2 Add wine and boil for 2–3 minutes, until reduced by more than half. Mix in tomato
   purée, stock and seasoning. Return to the boil, reduce heat and simmer, uncovered,
   for 2–2½ hours, stirring occasionally. Add 2 tablespoons of milk whenever the
   sauce starts to dry out.

3 Cook pasta in a large pan of boiling water, until al dente. Drain, transfer to a serving
   bowl and spoon over the sauce. Toss to combine, garnish with parmesan and serve.

NUTRITIONAL VALUE PER SERVE	FAT 9.1 G	CARBOHYDRATE 22 G	PROTEIN 10.7 G

Ham and cheese tortellini with sage butter

INGREDIENTS

90 g (3 oz) butter
1 clove garlic, crushed
20 fresh sage leaves, finely chopped
salt and black pepper
600 g (1¼ lb) fresh ham and cheese
   tortellini
60 g (2 oz) parmesan, grated
extra parmesan to serve
serves 4

PREPARATION TIME
10 minutes

COOKING TIME
15 minutes

1 Melt butter in a small pan, add garlic and sage, and sauté on a low heat for 1–2 minutes. Season with salt and pepper.

2 Cook pasta in a large pan of boiling water, until al dente. Drain and set aside.

3 Place tortellini in a large serving bowl, pour in butter sauce and parmesan, toss well to combine. Garnish with extra parmesan.

NUTRITIONAL VALUE PER SERVE	FAT **17.8** G	CARBOHYDRATE **11** G	PROTEIN **11.5** G

Meatballs with tomato sauce

INGREDIENTS

50 g (2 oz) fresh white breadcrumbs
500 g (1 lb) minced beef
2 rashers bacon, finely chopped
1 onion, chopped
3 tablespoons chopped fresh parsley
1 egg, beaten
sea salt
freshly ground black pepper
2 tablespoons sunflower oil
400 g (13 oz) jar garlic pasta sauce
400 g (13 oz) dried pasta (tagliatelle
   or penne)
extra parsley to garnish
serves 4

PREPARATION TIME
15 minutes, plus 10
minutes refrigeration

COOKING TIME
25 minutes

1 Place breadcrumbs in a large bowl, combine with beef, bacon, onion,
   parsley, egg and seasoning, and mix well. Roll into 20 balls and flatten
   slightly with the palm of your hand. Refrigerate for 10 minutes.

2 Heat oil in a frying pan and, over a medium-high heat, cook meatballs
   in batches, until browned on both sides. Drain off excess oil, pour
   pasta sauce over meatballs. Reduce heat and simmer for 10 minutes,
   turning occasionally, until cooked through.

3 Cook pasta in boiling water until al dente, and drain. Serve meatballs
   with pasta and garnish with extra parsley.

NUTRITIONAL VALUE PER SERVE	FAT 5.3 G	CARBOHYDRATE 21 G	PROTEIN 11 G

Macaroni with lamb ragoût

INGREDIENTS

2 tablespoons olive oil
4 tablespoons butter
1 stick celery, finely chopped
1 onion, finely chopped
1 small carrot, finely chopped
360 g (12 oz) minced lamb
1 cup (250 ml, 8 fl oz) milk
400 g (13 oz) dried macaroni
2 tablespoons chopped fresh mint
parmesan, grated

serves 4

PREPARATION TIME
15 minutes

COOKING TIME
20 minutes

1 Heat oil and butter in a large frying pan. Gently fry celery, onion and carrot for 5–7 minutes, until softened. Add lamb and cook, stirring, for 5–6 minutes, until meat has browned. Season.

2 Reduce heat to very low, stir in milk a little at a time, until milk is absorbed with each addition, and mixture is cooked through.

3 Cook pasta in a large pan of boiling water, until al dente. Drain. Serve pasta with sauce, garnish with mint and sprinkle with extra parmesan.

NUTRITIONAL VALUE PER SERVE	FAT **11.3** G	CARBOHYDRATE **22** G	PROTEIN **9.9** G

Tagliatelle with asparagus and prosciutto

INGREDIENTS

500 g (1 lb) asparagus
4 tablespoons unsalted butter
2 tablespoons olive oil
1 spring onion (green onion), sliced
60 g (2 oz) prosciutto, cut into strips
150 ml (5 fl oz) double cream
salt and black pepper
500 g (1 lb) fresh tagliatelle
parmesan, grated
serves 4

PREPARATION TIME
10 minutes

COOKING TIME
20 minutes

1 Cut asparagus spears into 3 cm (1 in) pieces. Heat butter and oil in a large frying pan, add spring onions (green onions), cook for 2 minutes to soften, stir in prosciutto. Cook for 2 minutes, add asparagus and cook for 5 minutes, until softened. Pour in cream and bring to the boil, season to taste.

2 Cook pasta in a large pan of boiling water, until al dente. Drain and transfer to serving bowl, pour over the sauce. Sprinkle with parmesan.

NUTRITIONAL VALUE PER SERVE	FAT **13.1** G	CARBOHYDRATE **26** G	PROTEIN **7** G

Meat ravioli with cream and parmesan

INGREDIENTS

600 g (1¼ lb) fresh beef ravioli
220 ml (7½ fl oz) double cream
2 tablespoons butter
freshly grated nutmeg
60 g (2 oz) parmesan, grated
salt and black pepper
extra parmesan to serve
serves 4

1 Cook ravioli in a large pan of boiling water, until al dente. Place half the cream and the butter in a large frying pan. Heat gently for 1 minute or until butter has melted.

2 Drain ravioli, add immediately to cream and butter mixture. Cook for 30 seconds, stirring. Mix in remaining cream, nutmeg and parmesan. Season and toss for a few seconds, until well combined and heated through. Serve with extra parmesan.

PREPARATION TIME
10 minutes

COOKING TIME
15 minutes

NUTRITIONAL VALUE PER SERVE	FAT **16.3** G	CARBOHYDRATE **14** G	PROTEIN **7** G

Gnocchi with pork and capsicums

INGREDIENTS

360 g (12 oz) pork steak, cubed
4 cloves garlic, crushed
1 tablespoon dried oregano
juice of ½ lemon
½ cup (125 ml, 4 fl oz) extra virgin
  olive oil
salt and black pepper
1 small onion, finely chopped
½ stick celery, finely chopped
3 tablespoons finely chopped
  fresh parsley
250 g (8 oz) yellow capsicums
  (peppers), chopped
220 ml (7½ fl oz) tomato paste
3 tablespoons beef stock
800 g (1 lb 10 oz) fresh gnocchi
25 g (1 oz) pitted black olives, sliced
serves 4

1 Place pork in a shallow, non-metallic dish. Mix in half the garlic, the oregano, lemon juice, 1 tablespoon of oil and seasoning. Cover and refrigerate for 1 hour.

2 Heat remaining oil in a large pan. Add onion and a pinch of salt. Cook for 5 minutes until softened. Stir in remaining garlic, celery, parsley and capsicums (peppers), and cook over a low heat for 10 minutes.

3 Stir in the tomato paste and simmer for a further 10 minutes, stirring often. Add pork, marinade and stock. Simmer, uncovered, for 10 minutes or until thickened and cooked through, stirring occasionally.

4 Cook gnocchi in a large pan of boiling water, until al dente. Drain and transfer to a large serving bowl. Spoon over the sauce and toss to combine. Sprinkle with olives.

PREPARATION TIME
20 minutes

COOKING TIME
35 minutes, plus
1 hour marinating

| NUTRITIONAL VALUE PER SERVE | FAT 7.4 G | CARBOHYDRATE 14 G | PROTEIN 7.4 G |

Spaghettini and scallops with breadcrumbs

INGREDIENTS

400 g (13 oz) dried spaghettini
12 fresh scallops with their corals
½ cup (125 ml, 4 fl oz) extra virgin
  olive oil
50 g (2 oz) fresh breadcrumbs
4 tablespoons chopped flat-leaf
  parsley
2 cloves garlic, crushed
1 teaspoon dried chillies, crushed
½ cup (125 ml, 4 fl oz) dry white wine
serves 4

PREPARATION TIME
10 minutes

COOKING TIME
15 minutes

1 Cook spaghettini in a large pan of boiling water, until al dente. Drain well and set
   aside.

2 Detach corals from scallops and set aside. Slice scallops into 3 or 4 pieces. Heat
   2 tablespoons of oil in a frying pan, add breadcrumbs and fry, stirring, until golden.
   Remove from pan and set aside.

3 Heat remaining oil in the pan, add 2 tablespoons of parsley, the garlic and chilli.
   Cook for 2 minutes.

4 Add scallops and cook for 30 seconds, until starting to turn opaque. Add wine and the
   reserved corals, cook for a further 30 seconds, add spaghettini and cook for 1 minute,
   tossing to heat through. Sprinkle with breadcrumbs and remaining parsley.

NUTRITIONAL VALUE PER SERVE	FAT 13.7 G	CARBOHYDRATE 35 G	PROTEIN 8.5 G

Linguine with prawns and scallops

INGREDIENTS

400 g (13 oz) linguine
1 kg (2 lb) tomatoes
olive oil, for drizzling
salt and pepper
90 ml (3 fl oz) olive oil
2 brown onions, chopped
3 garlic cloves, crushed
220 g (7$^1/_2$ oz) firm white fish fillet,
 cut into cubes
150 g (5 oz) calamari (squid), cut into
 rings
220 g (7$^1/_2$ oz) scallops
220 g (7$^1/_2$ oz) green prawns
 (shrimps), peeled
1 tablespoon tomato paste, optional
$^1/_3$ cup (90 ml, 3 fl oz) water
2 tablespoons chopped fresh parsley
parmesan, grated
serves 4

PREPARATION TIME
15 minutes

COOKING TIME
1 hour 10 minutes

1 Preheat oven to 180°C (350°F, gas mark 4).

2 Cook linguine in a large pan of boiling water, until al dente. Drain, set aside and keep warm. Cut the tomatoes in half and place on a baking tray. Drizzle with olive oil, sprinkle with salt and pepper, and roast in oven for 40–45 minutes. Cool slightly.

3 Place cooked tomatoes in a food processor and process until tomatoes are finely pulped.

4 Heat oil in a large pan, sauté onion and garlic until lightly coloured. Add fish, tossing gently for 1–2 minutes. Add calamari, cook 1 minute, add scallops and prawns, cook a further minute. Add tomato mixture, tomato paste and water and simmer for 5–10 minutes, making sure not to overcook seafood. Season with salt and pepper, stir through parsley. Serve with linguine and garnish with parmesan.

NUTRITIONAL VALUE PER SERVE	FAT **3.8** G	CARBOHYDRATE **12** G	PROTEIN **7.9** G

Chicken and mushroom linguine

INGREDIENTS

1 tablespoon sunflower oil
500 g (1 lb) chicken breast fillet,
 cut into 4 portions
6 cloves garlic, unpeeled
250 g (8 oz) brown cap mushrooms
 or wild mushrooms
220 ml (7½ fl oz) double cream
salt and black pepper
500 g (1 lb) fresh linguine
3 tablespoons butter
125 g (4 oz) parmesan, grated
serves 4

PREPARATION TIME
20 minutes

COOKING TIME
30 minutes

1 Preheat oven to 200°C (400°F, gas mark 6). Heat oil in a large
 frying pan, add chicken and fry for 1 minute on each side, until
 browned. Place in an ovenproof dish.

2 Add garlic cloves to the pan, fry for 3 minutes until softened.
 Remove from pan, leave to cool slightly, peel, mash and add to
 chicken with mushrooms, cream and seasoning. Cover dish with
 foil and bake for 20 minutes until cooked.

3 Cook pasta in a large pan of boiling water, until al dente. Drain,
 return to the pan, toss with butter and parmesan. Serve linguine
 topped with chicken and mushroom mixture.

NUTRITIONAL VALUE PER SERVE	FAT **15.3** G	CARBOHYDRATE **20** G	PROTEIN **12.8** G

Italian chicken pasta toss

INGREDIENTS

185 g (6 oz) dried pasta ribbons

1 tablespoon oil

2 cloves garlic, crushed

250 g (8 oz) chicken breast fillets,
    cut into strips

1 small onion, chopped

1 courgette (zucchini), sliced

1 small red capsicum (pepper),
    cut into strips

90 g (3 oz) frozen peas

1 teaspoon salt

1 teaspoon dried Italian seasoning

2 tomatoes, seeded and chopped

1 tablespoon grated parmesan

serves 4–6

1 Cook pasta in a large pan of boiling water, until
   al dente. Drain and set aside.

2 Heat oil in a large frying pan, add garlic and
   chicken. Stir-fry on a medium heat for
   5 minutes. Add onion, courgette (zucchini), red
   capsicum (pepper), peas, salt and seasoning,
   and stir-fry a further 2 minutes. Add tomatoes,
   stirring for 1–2 minutes to heat through.
   Remove from heat, add pasta, tossing to
   combine. Sprinkle with parmesan.

PREPARATION TIME
20 minutes

COOKING TIME
25 minutes

NUTRITIONAL VALUE PER SERVE	FAT **1.7** G	CARBOHYDRATE **12** G	PROTEIN **7.7** G

Rigatoni with turkey and sage ragoût

INGREDIENTS

2 tablespoons olive oil
1 onion, finely chopped
1 small red chilli, deseeded and
  finely chopped
1 green capsicum (pepper), chopped
500 g (1 lb) minced turkey
220 g (7 oz) can chopped tomatoes
1 tablespoon tomato purée
salt and black pepper
50 g (2 oz) pitted black olives, sliced
2 tablespoons chopped fresh sage
500 g (1 lb) fresh rigatoni
serves 4

1 Heat oil in a large pan. Gently cook onion, chilli and capsicum (pepper), stirring, for 5 minutes until softened.

2 Add turkey mince, stirring to separate mince, and cook over medium-high heat for 5 minutes, until browned. Add tomatoes, tomato purée and seasoning. Cover, reduce·heat and simmer for 20 minutes. Stir in olives and half of the sage. Simmer for 2–3 minutes.

3 Cook the pasta in a large pan of boiling water, until al dente. Drain well, add to sauce and toss gently. Serve sprinkled with remaining sage.

PREPARATION TIME
15 minutes

COOKING TIME
35 minutes

NUTRITIONAL VALUE PER SERVE	FAT **4.1** G	CARBOHYDRATE **25.5** G	PROTEIN **13.2** G

Glossary

Al dente: Italian term to describe pasta and rice that are cooked until tender but still firm to the bite.

Bake blind: to bake pastry cases without their fillings. Line the raw pastry case with greaseproof paper and fill with raw rice or dried beans to prevent collapsed sides and puffed base. Remove paper and fill 5 minutes before completion of cooking time.

Baste: to spoon hot cooking liquid over food at intervals during cooking to moisten and flavour it.

Beat: to make a mixture smooth with rapid and regular motions using a spatula, wire whisk or electric mixer; to make a mixture light and smooth by enclosing air.

Beurre manié: equal quantities of butter and flour mixed together to a smooth paste and stirred bit by bit into a soup, stew or sauce while on the heat to thicken. Stop adding when desired thickness results.

Bind: to add egg or a thick sauce to hold ingredients together when cooked.

Blanch: to plunge some foods into boiling water for less than a minute and immediately plunge into iced water. This is to brighten the colour of some vegetables and to remove skin from tomatoes and nuts.

Blend: to mix 2 or more ingredients thoroughly together; do not confuse with blending in an electric blender.

Boil: to cook in a liquid brought to boiling point and kept there.

Boiling point: when bubbles rise continually and break over the entire surface of the liquid, reaching a temperature of 100°C (212°F). In some cases food is held at this high temperature for a few seconds then heat is turned to low for slower cooking. See *simmer*.

Bouquet garni: a bundle of several herbs tied together with string for easy removal, placed into pots of stock, soups and stews for flavour. A few sprigs of fresh thyme, parsley and bay leaf are used. Can be purchased in sachet form for convenience.

Caramelise: to heat sugar in a heavy-based pan until it liquefies and develops a caramel colour. Vegetables such as blanched carrots and sautéed onions may be sprinkled with sugar and caramelised.

Chill: to place in the refrigerator or stir over ice until cold.

Clarify: to make a liquid clear by removing sediments and impurities. To melt fat and remove any sediment.

Coat: to dust or roll food items in flour to cover the surface before the food is cooked. Also, to coat in flour, egg and breadcrumbs.

Cool: to stand at room temperature until some or all heat is removed, eg cool a little, cool completely.

Cream: to make creamy and fluffy by working the mixture with the back of a wooden spoon; usually refers to creaming butter and sugar or margarine. May also be done with an electric mixer.

Croutons: small cubes of bread, toasted or fried, used as an addition to salads or as a garnish to soups and stews.

Crudités: raw vegetable sticks served with a dipping sauce.

Crumb: to coat foods in flour, egg and breadcrumbs to form a protective coating for foods which are fried. Also adds flavour and texture and enhances appearance.

Cube: to cut into small pieces with six even sides, eg cubes of meat.

Cut in: to combine fat, such as butter or shortening, and flour using 2 knives scissor-fashion or a pastry blender, to make pastry.

Deglaze: to dissolve dried-out cooking juices left on the base and sides of a roasting dish or frying pan. Add a little water, wine or stock, scrape and stir over heat until dissolved. Resulting liquid is used to make a flavoursome gravy or added to a sauce or casserole.

Degrease: to skim fat from the surface of cooking liquids, eg stocks, soups, casseroles.

Dice: to cut into small cubes.

Dredge: to heavily coat with icing sugar, sugar, flour or cornflour.

Dressing: a mixture added to completed dishes to add moisture and flavour, eg salads, cooked vegetables.

Drizzle: to pour in a fine thread-like stream moving over a surface.

Egg wash: beaten egg with milk or water used to brush over pastry, bread dough or biscuits to give a sheen and golden brown colour.

Essence: a strong flavouring liquid, usually made by distillation. Only a few drops are needed to flavour.

Fillet: a piece of prime meat, fish or poultry which is boneless or has all bones removed.

Flake: to separate cooked fish into flakes, removing any bones and skin, using 2 forks.

Flame: to ignite warmed alcohol over food or to pour into a pan with food, ignite, then serve.

Flute: to make decorative indentations around the pastry rim before baking.

Fold in: combining of a light, whisked or creamed mixture with other ingredients. Add a portion of the other ingredients at a time and mix using a gentle circular motion, over and under the mixture so that air will not be lost. Use a metal spoon or spatula.

Glaze: to brush or coat food with a liquid that will give the finished product a glossy appearance, and on baked products, a golden brown colour.

Grease: to rub the surface of a metal or heatproof dish with oil or fat, to prevent the food from sticking.

Herbed butter: softened butter mixed with finely chopped fresh herbs and re-chilled. Used to serve on grilled meats and fish.

Hors d'oeuvre: small savoury foods served as an appetiser, popularly known today as 'finger food'.

Infuse: to steep foods in a liquid until the liquid absorbs their flavour.

Joint: to cut poultry and game into serving pieces by dividing at the joint.

Julienne: to cut some food, eg vegetables and processed meats, into fine strips the length of matchsticks. Used in salads or as a garnish to cooked dishes.

Knead: to work a yeast dough in a pressing, stretching and folding motion with the heel of the hand until smooth and elastic to develop the gluten strands. Non-yeast doughs should be lightly and quickly handled as gluten development is not desired.

Line: to cover the inside of a baking tin with paper for the easy removal of the cooked product from the baking tin.

Macerate: to stand fruit in a syrup, liqueur or spirit to give added flavour.

Marinade: a flavoured liquid, into which food is placed for some time to give it flavour and to tenderise. Marinades include an acid ingredient such as vinegar or wine, oil and seasonings.

Mask: to evenly cover cooked food portions with a sauce, mayonnaise or savoury jelly.

Pan-fry: to fry foods in a small amount of fat or oil, sufficient to coat the base of the pan.

Parboil: to boil until partially cooked. The food is then finished by some other method.

Pare: to peel the skin from vegetables and fruit. 'Peel' is the popular term but 'pare' is the name given to the knife used; paring knife.

Pit: to remove stones or seeds from olives, cherries, dates.

Pith: the white lining between the rind and flesh of oranges, grapefruit and lemons.

Pitted: the olives, cherries, dates etc. with the stone removed, eg purchase pitted dates.

Poach: to simmer gently in enough hot liquid to almost cover the food so its shape will be retained.

Pound: to flatten meats with a meat mallet; to reduce to a paste or small particles with a mortar and pestle.

Simmer: to cook in liquid just below boiling point at about 96°C (205°F) with small bubbles rising gently to the surface.

Skim: to remove fat or froth from the surface of simmering food.

Stock: the liquid produced when meat, poultry, fish or vegetables have been simmered in water to extract the flavour. Used as a base for soups, sauces, casseroles etc. Convenience stock products are available.

Sweat: to cook sliced onions or vegetables in a small amount of butter in a covered pan over low heat, to soften them and release flavour without colouring.

Conversions

Measurements differ from country to country, so it's important to understand what the differences are. This Measurements Guide gives you simple 'at-a-glance' information for using the recipes in this book, wherever you may be.

Cooking is not an exact science – minor variations in measurements won't make a difference to your cooking.

EQUIPMENT

There is a difference in the size of measuring cups used internationally, but the difference is minimal (only 2–3 teaspoons). We use the Australian standard metric measurements in our recipes:

1 teaspoon.....5 ml   1 tablespoon.....20 ml
½ cup.....125 ml   1 cup.....250 ml
4 cups.....1 litre

Measuring cups come in sets of one cup (250 ml), ½ cup (125 ml), ⅓ cup (80 ml) and ¼ cup (60 ml). Use these for measuring liquids and certain dry ingredients.

Measuring spoons come in a set of four and should be used for measuring dry and liquid ingredients.

When using cup or spoon measures, always make them level (unless the recipe indicates otherwise).

DRY VERSUS WET INGREDIENTS

While this system of measures is consistent for liquids, it's more difficult to quantify dry ingredients. For instance, one level cup equals: 200 g of brown sugar; 210 g of caster sugar; and 110 g of icing sugar.

When measuring dry ingredients such as flour, don't push the flour down or shake it into the cup. It is best just to spoon the flour in until it reaches the desired amount. When measuring liquids, use a clear vessel indicating metric levels.

Always use medium eggs (55–60 g) when eggs are required in a recipe.

OVEN

Your oven should always be at the right temperature before placing the food in it to be cooked. Note that if your oven doesn't have a fan you may need to cook food for a little longer.

MICROWAVE

It is difficult to give an exact cooking time for microwave cooking. It is best to watch what you are cooking closely to monitor its progress.

STANDING TIME

Many foods continue to cook when you take them out of the oven or microwave. If a recipe states that the food needs to 'stand' after cooking, be sure not to overcook the dish.

CAN SIZES

The can sizes available in your supermarket or grocery store may not be the same as specified in the recipe. Don't worry if there is a small variation in size – it's unlikely to make a difference to the end result.

dry		liquids	
metric (grams)	imperial (ounces)	metric (millilitres)	imperial (fluid ounces)
		30 ml	1 fl oz
30 g	1 oz	60 ml	2 fl oz
60 g	2 oz	90 ml	3 fl oz
90 g	3 oz	100 ml	3 1/2 fl oz
100 g	3 1/2 oz	125 ml	4 fl oz
125 g	4 oz	150 ml	5 fl oz
150 g	5 oz	190 ml	6 fl oz
185 g	6 oz	250 ml	8 fl oz
200 g	7 oz	300 ml	10 fl oz
250 g	8 oz	500 ml	16 fl oz
280 g	9 oz	600 ml	20 fl oz (1 pint)*
315 g	10 oz	1000 ml (1 litre)	32 fl oz
330 g	11 oz		
370 g	12 oz		
400 g	13 oz		
440 g	14 oz		
470 g	15 oz		
500 g	16 oz (1 lb)		
750 g	24 oz (1 1/2 lb)		
1000 g (1 kg)	32 oz (2 lb)		*Note: an American pint is 16 fl oz.

cooking temperatures	°C (celsius)	°F (fahrenheit)	gas mark
very slow	120	250	1/2
slow	150	300	2
moderately slow	160	315	2–3
moderate	180	350	4
moderately hot	190	375	5
	200	400	6
hot	220	425	7
very hot	230	450	8
	240	475	9
	250	500	10

Index

Essential COOKING SERIES

COMPREHENSIVE, STEP-BY-STEP COOKING

Essential COOKING SERIES
COMPREHENSIVE, STEP-BY-STEP COOKING
Baking

Essential COOKING SERIES
COMPREHENSIVE, STEP-BY-STEP COOKING
Chicken Meals

Essential COOKING SERIES
COMPREHENSIVE, STEP-BY-STEP COOKING
Salads & Greens

Essential COOKING SERIES
COMPREHENSIVE, STEP-BY-STEP COOKING
Soups & Hors D'Oeuvres

Essential COOKING SERIES
COMPREHENSIVE, STEP-BY-STEP COOKING
Meat Dishes

Essential COOKING SERIES
COMPREHENSIVE, STEP-BY-STEP COOKING
Finger Food

Essential COOKING SERIES
COMPREHENSIVE, STEP-BY-STEP COOKING
Pasta Dishes

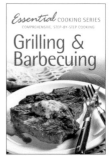

Essential COOKING SERIES
COMPREHENSIVE, STEP-BY-STEP COOKING
Grilling & Barbecuing

Essential COOKING SERIES
COMPREHENSIVE, STEP-BY-STEP COOKING
Rice & Risotto

Essential COOKING SERIES
COMPREHENSIVE, STEP-BY-STEP COOKING
Vegetarian Dishes

Essential COOKING SERIES
COMPREHENSIVE, STEP-BY-STEP COOKING
Asian Dishes

Essential COOKING SERIES
COMPREHENSIVE, STEP-BY-STEP COOKING
Stir-Fry